W9-AAE-309

Introduction

When I began studying the martial arts back in 1972, the whole subject was shrouded in mystery; indeed, that was part of the attraction. At that time there was only a limited range of books on the subject and therefore very little information was available to the novice.

I am glad to say that this has changed in recent years beyond all recognition. With the explosion of interest in the martial arts and the vast array of quality books that are now on the market, we seem to be increasing our knowledge and understanding of the martial arts and sports science, and this fact is reflected in this new series of books.

Over the past 30 years, I have been privileged to compete, train, and teach with practitioners from most of the disciplines covered in this series. I have coached world champions, developed and adapted training methods for people with disabilities, and instructed members of the armed forces in close-quarter techniques. I can warmly recommend this series as a rich source of information for students and instructors alike. Books can never replace a good instructor and club, but the student who does not study when the training is finished will never progress.

Aidan Trimble—Sixth Dan, Former World Karate Champion

Shocking examples of breaking are common to modern-day martial arts. Although this practice is highly dangerous and should only ever be attempted by highly trained experts, the level of concentration and power of the mind over matter is impressive.

The Nonphysical Aims of Martial Arts

Oriental martial arts are almost as varied as the people who practice them. Well-known martial arts, such as judo, karate, kung fu, jujutsu, taekwondo, and kickboxing, have enough practitioners in the West to make a nation-state of several million people. And despite the decline of traditional martial arts in China and their replacement with wu shu—a kind of acrobatic martial gymnastics—there are millions of Chinese people actively engaged in related arts today.

Unfortunately, because these arts have largely been classified and promoted as methods of staying in shape, or as sports, self-defense, or performance arts, teachers and promoters have overemphasized physical and technical development at the expense of the philosophical, mental, and spiritual teachings these arts also offer.

A martial arts master once asked his students, "Which is more important, the body or the mind?" Because the subject was martial arts, some students thought that the body, or rather what it could do, was most important. Others thought that the mind was more important. No one realized that it was a trick question.

"How can a body do anything without a mind?" asked the master. "And,

Composure, serenity, and dignity are hallmarks of the state of mind known in Japanese as "zanshin," or remaining mind, demonstrated here by this swordsman.

practices, Musashi developed intense powers of concentration. He gained the upper hand in some 60 contests, allegedly even winning one contest with an improvised sword that was really a boat paddle. Musashi was so successful because he developed a formidable spirit, a strong will, and always held the "mental edge," a term used in this book to describe the advantages of superior and focused concentration, and a part of the nonphysical aspects of the martial arts.

Many books about martial arts deal with the techniques and the history.

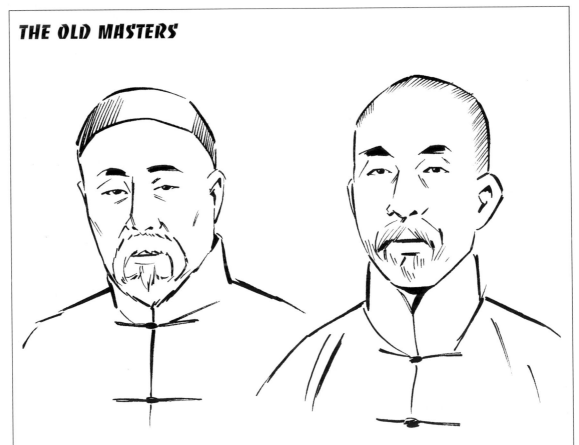

THE OLD MASTERS

Master Li Ts'un-I (left) and Master Sun Lu-Tang (right) were contemporaries and famous masters of pa-kua. It was said of Master Sun Lu-Tang that "his eyes were very high," meaning he understood and could perform pa-kua to an exceedingly high standard.

Few examine the nonphysical benefits of martial arts or approach them as a tool for spiritual or mental, as opposed to physical, development. However, there is much to be gained from studying these nonphysical aspects. Martial arts can act as a vehicle to develop and demonstrate, for example, the complete focus of concentration referred to as the "mental edge."

The mental edge is used here to describe the skill of, for example, a top tennis player who loses the first set but still wins the match. Sometimes, the outcome of a contest between two equally matched combatants is decided in the minds of the combatants. In such cases, the winner undoubtedly had the mental edge.

Developing the mental edge is not a substitute for skill, technique, and effort, it merely enhances them. In a practical sense then, the well-developed mind of the martial artist is used in conjunction with the well-trained body.

CHINESE MONASTERIES: CENTERS OF EXCELLENCE

During China's long history, its people have produced many noted centers of excellence and learning. However, there is one that concerns us above all others. It is the famed Shaolin Temple of Honan Province, the birthplace of Chan (Zen) Buddhism and home of the Chinese martial arts. The monks and nuns of the Shaolin Temple practiced and taught martial arts as part of a philosophical, spiritual, and **holistic** way of life that also included the healing arts.

The martial art taught at the Shaolin Temple was kung fu, which uses deflecting, blocking, punching, striking, kicking, seizing, grappling, and throwing techniques, as well as traditional Chinese weapons, like the

Zen Buddhists believe that everything constantly changes, so they practice opening themselves up to the flow of life without trying to hang on to the past or manipulate the future.

spear and the long pole. Kung fu is a Cantonese Chinese word meaning "hard work."

The relevance of the Shaolin Temple lies in the traditions maintained among many Oriental arts that the Shaolin Temple is the home of Chinese martial arts, and that these were an undoubted influence on the martial arts of other Eastern countries, like Japan and Korea. This tradition, however, does not take into consideration the fact that combative and self-defense techniques already existed in China long before the founding of the Shaolin Temple.

Martial arts historians argue to this day about the specific role that the Shaolin Temple played in the development of martial arts in general; however, I agree with the martial artist and historian Patrick McCarthy when he says:

"It would be ludicrous to even consider that self-defense methods did not exist in ancient China prior to the advent of the Shaolin order; however, the advent and subsequent development of a codified self-defense system with spiritual characteristics and a moral philosophy with which to govern the behavior of those who mastered its secrets, remains purely a cultural phenomenon cradled in the confines of austere Chinese monastic sanctuaries."

(From European seminar records sent to the author in 1995.)

To which I would add: the philosophical base of the martial arts developed at the Shaolin Temple has a great deal to offer young people today. Because the chief interest of the Shaolin monks and nuns lay in developing and practicing meditation techniques, they placed a heavy emphasis on methods of concentration. Some of theses techniques are perfect for developing the mental edge that, once learned, can spread out into all aspects of a young person's life. There are also many other benefits of a noncombative nature to be gained from martial arts practice. Such benefits can be labeled as non-utility, meaning they do not pertain directly to combat or self-defense.

the Chinese terms "qigong" (chi kung) and gongfu (kung fu). Indeed, the depth of such a concept as "gong" is immediately apparent whenever a serious student engages in such a practice as the Fujianese health-based martial arts.

The Fujianese animal exercises involve qigong (inner or internal self-defense) and gongfu self-protection concepts (outer self-defense, often misconstrued as fighting skills) as well as medium-speed movements that promote circulation of both blood and **chi** (internal life force). Such exercises can be maintained for the duration of one's life, and this is an intelligent use of traditional Chinese medicine, which promotes a long and healthy life.

The proof of this is evident when one considers that Fujian Province is renowned for the high number of individuals who are well into their first century of life. My main master has recently celebrated his 98th year of life and his 80th of teaching!

The animal exercises have been taken to new heights since Dr. Hua To's concept of animal imitation 2,000 years ago. Dr. To was a famous Chinese physician who

YIN AND YANG

The circular diagram shown here is known as yin and yang. It is used to illustrate polarity, meaning that everything has an opposite. There is no up without down, or hot without cold, black without white, etc. Following on from this, it can be said that there is no life without death.

Buddhist statues and images, beautiful works of art in their own right, are used to capture teaching gestures, body postures, ritual gestures, and to act as a focus for attention. They are not "worshipped" as such.

discovered the concept of anaesthesia. His animal exercises now serve as the ultimate in self-help therapy and natural mind and body science. Self-defense skills represent only a small portion of the overall picture.

The animal exercises of Fujian are a pre-karate art form acknowledging all aspects of ancient Chinese culture, including obvious and serious links to Daoism (Taoism), Buddhism, and Confucianism. The exercises of Fujian are nonviolent expressions of both inner and outer self-defense, the former

Intelligence Grows in a Healthy Mind

What is the mind? The mind is something that can easily be misunderstood, and if we try to think about the mind, the first problem we come up with is where to locate it. That might sound a bit odd at first, but let us ask the question more clearly: where is the mind? Easy, you might say, it is in your head. Well, no, not really. Your brain is in your head, but an old argument, debated among scholars and wise people for many hundreds of years, claims that the mind (like the soul) cannot be seen. So, what is the mind?

This issue can get quite confusing, but the important and useful point here is that if we (temporarily) separate the mind from the brain, we can recognize that humans have a mental ability that other animals do not. Animals, like humans, have brains, but animals act purely on programmed instincts, and the choices they make are limited by the inbuilt programs of their species. Mice do not act like tigers. So, for cats and dogs, for example, there is no real right or wrong, no theft, crime, punishment, or religion. They cannot rise above or go beyond their instincts. Humans, however, can. Even to the point of planning and carrying out an act that will ultimately

A picture of tranquility. "Gently the water flows, but how great is the strength concealed within? The furious current is too difficult to stop. It envelops the rocks with a wave...Water overcomes all!" (A tai chi saying.)

To attain mastery in swordsmanship, it was necessary for samurai warriors to transcend, or go beyond, death while still alive. In order to do this, they received mind training in riddles that can be tricky to understand.

lead to their own death. This point is explained by the practices of Japan's historical warrior elite, the **samurai**. They operated through a code of conduct called bushido, or the way of the warrior.

BUSHIDO

The way of the warrior in ancient Japan was a narrow and tough path to follow. The samurai were the elite warrior caste of Japan between the 13th and 19th centuries—a period of more than 600 years. During that time, many tales of the bravery (and sometimes the bloody brutality) of the samurai were collected and recorded. From our point of interest, which is the power of the mind, what is perhaps the most outstanding thing about the samurai was their legendary power to willingly face death for their cause, and to face that death while honorably and nobly doing their duty. They produced a standard code that strictly laid down how a samurai should live his life, discharge his duty to his lord, and ultimately, how he should die.

The most famous (and perhaps most unpleasant) type of death associated with the samurai was seppuku. Seppuku is often referred to as hara-kiri, or "belly cut." It is a ritually conducted suicide in which the samurai stabs or cuts his own stomach. Mercifully, the samurai usually had a second standing by—a trusty friend who would cut off the head of the mortally wounded man. There are many other accounts of hara-kiri, but they are too gruesome to recount here. Of more interest to our subject of the mind is the mind-set of a samurai committing seppuku and the determination to carry out such a willful act of self-destruction against all instincts for self-preservation.

One samurai ideal was to put duty (giri) before self-interest, health, wealth, or even family. And although I do not mean to suggest that anyone

ZANSHIN

Zanshin is a Japanese term that can be translated as "remaining mind." It is a useful concept for a martial artist to learn. Indeed, it is one of the principles or conditions that allows the mental edge to be used.

The remaining mind is the part of the mind that takes effective action once all mental distractions have been removed or bypassed. It is a common assumption that traditional martial arts require lots of aggression, but this is not so. Aggression is an emotive force operating in a mind that is not clear. A samurai would have claimed that, for a warrior with a well-trained mind, there should be no distinction "in terms of purity of action" between picking a flower and cutting down an enemy. There should simply be intention and action. According to the late Shoshine Nagamine, a famous classical karate master, "There should not be the thickness of a hair between a man's thought or word and his deed."

Zanshin, then, is the mind that remains (and works) when all emotions and distractions have been removed.

I always found zanshin rather difficult to understand, and I thought that not having any emotions sounded rather horrible and somehow inhuman. But now, I understand that zanshin is used in a worklike way by martial artists during their training, and not, for example, when enjoying a day out at the beach with their families.

The use of zanshin is not confined to martial artists. Champion athletes, boxers, gymnasts, and others use individual and personal approaches to achieve zanshin, although they do not call it such. They learn to shut out distractions and focus on the job at hand. I have referred to this ability elsewhere as the mental edge.

The final phase of a karate punch uses a process known as kime (pronounded kee-may). Kime means "focus," and refers to tightening the muscles supporting the arm to prevent the punch from bouncing off the target or collapsing.

Taekwondo (Korean karate) was inspired by Japanese karate, which was inspired by Okinawan karate, which in turn was inspired by Chinese kung fu, the common denominator among many Asian martial arts.

The whole Shaolin practice was designed to cultivate, increase, and demonstrate concentration; to improve and maintain health; and to foster nonviolent responses to force.

THE THREE Cs: CONCENTRATION, CALCULATION, AND COMMUNICATION

Concentration, calculation, and communication are three things essential in the process of education in general, and of learning martial arts in particular.

CONCENTRATION

Without concentration, you cannot take in information. Therefore, concentration is the cornerstone of learning. In martial arts fighting, lapses in concentration can be painful. You may get struck, punched, kicked, or thrown. Needless to say, if you are careless, you could injure either yourself or another.

CALCULATION

Calculation does not only refer to numbers. If you think deeply about what you are about to say to someone, and you succeed in saying exactly what you mean, you will have used the process of calculation—weighing things up— in this case, to make a calculated statement. Martial artists are required to make carefully calculated judgments, for instance, to determine the strategy of an opponent, to calculate his or her strengths and weaknesses, and to calculate the relative distance between themselves and an opponent in order to take the appropriate action. Good calculation and good judgement are born of good concentration.

COMMUNICATION

Communication takes place on many levels, but basically, it can be verbal, written, or gestured. Everything from a simple shrug of the shoulders to a formally written letter is scanned by the ever-curious human mind for information.

Humans are social creatures, and we base our lives around social groupings. These social groupings include our friends, but just on the edge of our particular social groupings exist our enemies, or at the very least, those people we do not like, or those people who do not like us. There is nothing wrong with the fact that you may not like someone or that someone might not like you. You cannot be friends with or like everyone, and you cannot realistically expect everyone to like you.

The real trick to learn here is communication. That is, how to keep your dignity and your "space" around those people you are less than comfortable with—and how to afford them theirs. These, and other practical and socially useful skills, like courtesy and respect, are learned and rehearsed in martial arts training halls, where they are practiced before, during, and after the challenges of controlled combat.

In a physical sense, true martial arts forms (choreographed sequences of movements) are messages in movement left to us by the masters. They physically record the exact techniques of a given martial art for communication, preservation, and demonstration.

TRAINING BEGINS AND ENDS WITH A BOW

Many of the avoidable problems that befall humankind are due to poor communication or a lack of it, in everything from a simple argument to a war. Martial arts training on the other hand teaches courtesy and respect and fosters dignity and the acceptance of the dignity of another, right from the start.

When you walk into the training hall, you are required to bow, to show respect for the training hall. A traditional bow should also be performed

Respect must be paid to your opponent because without him or her, you cannot remove yourself from the trap of self-limitation. Here, we see a traditional karate bow, or "rei."

Moving Meditation: Solo Forms

Martial arts masters have, for hundreds, perhaps thousands of years, recorded their experiences and techniques, not in books, but in sequences of physical movements.

These ancient forms have many different names to describe them (according to the martial art concerned), but collectively, they represent a rich and culturally diverse treasure-house of human martial arts experiences.

In kung fu, these sequences of movements are called **quan** (fist) or **hsing** (diagram). In karate, judo, and other Japanese martial arts, they are called kata (plan/program/form). In taekwondo, they are known as **hyung** (patterns).

Because of the vast numbers of these forms, I have selected advice and information on a single one only.

SANCHIN SOLO FORM

Many famous kung fu and karate masters have said that a great karate or kung fu master would not know more than three to five forms or kata. Some have even claimed one is enough.

One of the strategies in tai chi is to let your opponent come forward and to rotate with the force in response, without resisting or losing contact. You must be light and agile. When the opponent's force is spent, he or she is then open to a counterattack.

Sanchin ("three conflicts") is a solo kata that is shared by both kung fu and karate.

It is the root form for karate styles such as goju-ryu (hard-soft school) and ueichi-ryu (Ueichi family school), and for most Chinese crane styles. The sanchin kata bears so much similarity to other kung fu methods that I cannot help but agree with Chinese, Okinawan, and other teachers who have always claimed that "sanchin is everything."

According to Master Xia Bai Hua of the Beijing Wu Shu Research Institute in China, sanchin (also called san chien or san tzan) is the basic training form for many (if not most) of the Fujianese systems, the most prominent of which is the white crane school, which is a general term used to describe all crane-imitating boxing.

In Southern Shaolin Temple ancestors boxing, sanchin is both the basic and the advanced training.

White crane is a general term used to describe all crane-imitating boxing. Tradition maintains that it was created by the Shaolin monks. This view is supported by Patrick McCarthy, one of many prominent martial arts historians who support this view.

Dr. Yang Jwing Ming, a kung fu master and martial arts author, had this to say about the subject:

"The earliest reference we can find [for crane boxing] is the Shaolin."

The sanchin kata has several different sequences, which are followed by different schools, but the essence of all sequences is contained in the three sections into which the form is usually divided. The following is a simplified version often taught in the goju-ryu style of karate. The full version usually employs a series of turns.

The commitment of these young people to their technique demonstrates one of the values of martial arts training. If we seek control of the body using the mind, we must learn to work with the body and not seek to dominate it. Even the greatest expert cannot perform the impossible.

SANCHIN SECTION ONE

Assume the attention posture. Stand with your heels together and your hands at your sides, palms facing inward. Bring your feet together, and perform a traditional bow. Return to the attention posture. Breathe in, and then as you exhale, step out with your right leg and assume the sanchin position shown on page 58. Your shoulders should not move, and the angle of your elbows should be greater than 90 degrees, with both arms at the same height and in the same position. Push your hips forward. When you have completed the step and the exhalation, let your hips drop naturally back as you inhale while drawing your left fist to the side of your body.

your right shoulder with the fingers pointing up. Begin to exhale as you extend both hands forward. Do not straighten them completely. Keep your palms and fingers vertical and your elbows in. Push your hips forward, and complete your exhalation. Step back, and perform this technique on the opposite side (see page 63).

SECTION THREE SUMMARY

Sanchin is a whole-body exercise. In practicing its postures, steps, and physical movements, you should grip the floor with your feet. The "frame" made by this stance will exercise your ankles, knees, thighs, and buttocks. Provided you are not tense, the tight movements of section one will exercise the muscles at the side of your body (latissimus dorsi) as well as your chest, back, and upper-arm muscles. The movements in section two exercise the muscles under your arm between the elbow and the armpit (triceps) and also the shoulder (deltoid) and chest (pectoral) muscles. Section three opens the chest and back muscles, stretching them and the rib cage. Throughout the kata, the large-muscle groups controlling the diaphragm are continually employed to create a special kind of breathing that develops your ability to concentrate.

HARD AND SOFT

For many years, people have argued the merits of the hard, external style versus the soft, internal style in their approaches to the martial arts. The external school, it is claimed, relies on strength, speed, and power; and the internal school supposedly stresses softness, pliability, yielding, and the use of chi.

SANCHIN—SECTION 2

STEP 1: At the conclusion of Section 1, place both open hands in the sanchin position.

STEP 2: Turn your hands over, palms-down, with your elbows out.

STEP 3: Slowly withdraw both hands to the sides of the body, clenching your fists as you do so.

STEP 4: Open both hands and push your arms forward at solar plexus height.

STEP 5: Drop your hands back to reform the position in step 2.

In reality, both schools train to develop power; they simply use different methods. Mystical claims aside, it all amounts to the same thing: the generation and transmission of energy from point A to point B.

The question of hard and soft disappears if you do not generate or use your own power, but cultivate instead the ability to "borrow" a training partner's force.

HOW TO DEVELOP THE MENTAL EDGE

During kata practice, one becomes able to develop the mental edge by controlling the activity of the senses and removing fear and other interfering distractions. To practice removing distraction and to develop the mental edge, try the following technique.

The eyes look straight to the front and slightly down. Vision must be diffused. The ears must be "sealed." If sounds are heard, the distraction that they can produce must be quickly dealt with. The nose should be employed in inhaling. The tongue should be kept pressed to the hard palate of the mouth, and the jaw should not be clenched.

The skin should help register spatial awareness. Clothing should be loose and comfortable. The mind, now free from distraction, can concentrate completely on what it is doing, yet the whole body is working in a coordinated way.

TAI CHI

Tai chi has been mentioned already in this book, but I will give a broader description here.

Some people say that tai chi is a martial art, others that is merely for

SANCHIN—SECTION 3

STEP 1: At the conclusion of section 2, place your left hand under your right elbow and begin...

STEP 2: ...a circular sliding movement with your right hand moving across your chest.

STEP 3: Draw your right hand back and towards your shoulder and your left hand back and towards your waist.

STEP 4: Press both palms forward, making sure your elbows are kept in and remain bent. Repeat on the opposite side.

health. Yet more refer to it as moving-meditation breathing exercises or a physical means of expressing Chinese Taoist philosophy, which we will take a look at later.

Perhaps tai chi is all of the above and maybe more. It is up to you to make tai chi what you want it to be. Chinese people spent thousands of years studying the human body and mind, and the human ailments that affect both. One fact that they came up with is that the body and mind work best when they work in harmony, and this is one of the aims of tai chi. The art is normally taught in a long, flowing sequence of slow-motion movements that are beautiful to watch and pleasant to do. Tai chi will relax you, focus your mind, and promote creativity, sensitivity, and optimism.

One of the best things about tai chi is that virtually anyone can do it. You do not have to be fit, athletic, or even in shape to get some benefit from it. Neither do you have to be clever. You just have to learn the movements and practice them.

The creation of tai chi is a subject of much dispute and storytelling. One common story about the founding of tai chi involves the alleged founder, Chang San Feng, watching a fight between a snake and a crane and copying the defensive movements of the crane. Another tells of Chang San Feng rearing a huge ape and teaching it tai chi.

These colorful stories should not be seen simply as fanciful myths and legends, but rather as attempts to place the creation of tai chi in some golden age of heroes and to make tai chi a product of that age.

Left: This technique is referred to as "an" in tai chi. A tai chi saying suggests that the an technique is like the force of the river, which flows gently yet is mighty.

AIKIDO

Aikido is a modern Japanese martial art that is a synthesis of several more-traditional Japanese arts. Aikido can be translated as the "way of harmony spirit," or "(the) harmony spirit way." It is a modern manifestation of the Japanese martial arts, budo.

The founder of aikido, Master Morihei Ueshiba (1883–1969) dedicated himself to establishing a martial art that he felt would meet the needs of people living a modern world. Japan had, for centuries, been in a **feudal** state, and Japanese warriors could still be seen wearing swords in public as late as the 1860s. Master Ueshiba sought to preserve the spirit of budo rather than the letter. By this, I mean that aikido training differed from more-traditional martial arts in that it did not center on warrior culture and held no tournaments or competitions (although some modern aikido schools, notably the tomiki school, do).

Aikido stresses the use of wrist- and arm-locking techniques as well as throwing techniques.

TAOISM

Taoism (pronounced dow/tow-ism), blended with Buddhism, formed the basis for Zen, and it was from Zen that kung fu, karate, and other martial arts unfolded.

The most well-known Taoist teachers are Lao Tze and Chuang Tze. Lao Tze was born in Hu-Hsien in the state of Ch'u—what is now present-day

Right: An immobilization technique alongside a throwing technique is performed here in this aikido multiple-opponent scenario. In actual combat, however, defense against more than one opponent is extremely problematic.

Chuang Tze's teachings are filled with wisdom and humor. They deal with topics such as greed, ignorance, fear, false modesty, and false piety. Chaung Tze takes particular issue with those who break the laws of nature and the Tao.

Taoists cultivate quiet, non-action (not to be confused with laziness), and relaxation (not to be confused with idleness). They strive to live in the "now" and practice acceptance.

Imagine if you had everything, if nothing was missing. Imagine if you were everything, all things in you and you in them. This is to truly be one with the Tao, then, you/we would be complete.

The Taoist path is trodden by living vigorously in the now and by practicing acceptance. Here, the Taoist and Buddhist paths conjoin. I also find this truth reflected in the Christian doctrine of love.

The overall message of Taoism can perhaps be summed up in the concept called wu-wei.

WU-WEI

The Chinese concept of wu-wei (unmotivated action) cannot be understood by complicated explanations, because it is something that must be felt or experienced. From the perspective of the martial arts, however, the practical application of this philosophy results in several important benefits:

1. Fear and other unwanted emotions are prevented from interfering with

Left: Communication with nature has long been an element of Buddhist contemplation. Indeed, the original Buddhist monks were forest dwellers.

Pushing-Hands

Pushing-hands was created to develop good defensive skills, and is closely tied to "listening" techniques. Listening techniques are dependent on the sense of touch; they are used to read or determine an opponent's strengths and weaknesses, and also to determine the nature and direction of any attack.

"Be as a dragonfly that perches on the top of a stick raised to strike it." (Chinese proverb)

"In China, every style has pushing-hands. It doesn't matter which style. Firstly you have to get in touch with each other to learn sensitivity."
—Dr. Yang Jwing Ming (Fighting Arts International)

Here is an excerpt about pushing-hands in the Shaolin Temple. It is from the martial arts book *Barefoot Zen* and is concerned with the fictitious account of a young Shaolin monk named Chu:

"The session began with solo form practice, which was always conducted in the shade of the trees that surrounded the temple. It was believed that

Wing chun kung fu has a saying connected with the practice of sticking-hands, the wing chun version of pushing-hands. "Hand against hand, foot against foot, in kung fu, there is no unstoppable technique."

the trees would yield up their chi, or vital spirit, and that practice in such places was beneficial. Near flowing water was also considered to be a good location, but never near stagnant water; it was considered to cause a negative chi flow or even a blockage.

"With solo form practice complete, pushing-hands practice began. Chu was uncertain about this. He was still confined to the fixed-position variety and probably would be for several months to come. He preferred practicing with certain people, those with whom he got on. Others made him feel irritated and unskillful. He often tried to avoid them, but teachers Li and Tao Sheng always made him swap partners. He sometimes wondered if they were just getting at him. Later, he knew better. Eight months later, he began to learn the moving push hands, which had a greater variety of both movement and range.

"Life at the temple was strict and well-ordered, but relaxed. Novices and ordained monks and nuns arose and retired at the same times each day. They woke just before sunrise and retired just after sunset, taking only one communal meal per day, before noon. In the rainy season, they often meditated during the night and were free to sleep when they chose. The monks and nuns slept apart and led almost separate lives, except when they came together to hear the teachings, for seated meditation, and, of course, to practice breathing techniques, solo forms, and pushing-hands."

Pushing-hands methods vary considerably from style to style and from school to school. For example, white crane kung fu has a circular, horizontal type of pushing-hands, while tai chi has a backward and forward version.

Right: Once in contact, pushing-hands experts can rely on their sense of touch rather than vision. Indeed, at an advanced level, pushing-hands experts can practice while blindfolded.

PUSHING-HANDS

STEP 1: Begin pushing-hands in a relaxed but alert position with your forearms. You and your partner keep your forearms in contact.

STEP 2: As your partner begins to push towards the center, you momentarily hold him or her out before beginning to "yield."

The wing chun kung fu style, originally studied by Bruce Lee, has its own distinctive version of pushing-hands called chi sau, or sticking-hands.

During pushing- and sticking-hands practice, force is passed from one person to the other in an alternating pattern that grows in subtlety and complexity, depending on the skill of the practitioners.

The idea was to provide a method by which practitioners would have their state of mind, physical balance, and reflexes challenged by each other. When practicing pushing-hands, you should avoid "struggling" using force. Forces should be "blended" with, then neutralized and returned to the sender.

Pushing-hands methods include: pushing and changing hands; pressing and trapping hands; escaping hands; rolling arms; gripping hands; grip escapes; leg traps; leg presses; leg escapes; and advancing, retreating, and circle stepping.

More than just a separate exercise, the continuous action of pushing-hands is the original medium through which to express the techniques from traditional kung fu forms automatically by touch and without thinking. Remember, with pushing-hands you can feel what is going on and react instantly. Repetition is a part of learning to push hands, but the movement must never become routine.

Techniques to either attack or defend are triggered by contact, not by vision. Changes in circumstance are read automatically by the arms, which, acting like the antennae of an insect, remain in contact with the partner's arms and detect every movement. In wing chun kung fu, this is called sticking-hands.

KEEPING SILK

The quality of force used between pushing-hands opponents is referred to as "silk." This expression describes the desired evenness of tension that

FROM PUSHING-HANDS TO WRIST LOCKING

STEP 1: If your partner overextends his or her arm, he or she loses the power of leverage and becomes vulnerable to a wrist-locking technique.

STEP 2: Grip your partner's right wrist, as shown, and bend back the fingers against the wrist.

should be maintained when spinning silk. If the tension varies, then the thread will snap, the spinning will stop and start, and the finished silk will be lumpy and weak. If the thread tension is smoothly maintained, however, the spinning will be continuous, and the silk will be fine, even, and strong. This evenness of tension also applies to the practice of pushing-hands.

If force is met with force, conflict and chaos is all you will get, often with the biggest, strongest, or most-aggressive person winning. This is low-grade pushing-hands, if indeed, it can be called pushing-hands at all. Without a clear understanding of what you are doing, pushing-hands practice can turn into a crude wrestling match.

THE STRUCTURE OF PUSHING-HANDS

There are three distinct phases used in dealing with attacks during pushing-hands:

1. Detect (detecting a force)
2. Cling (intercepting, sticking to, and neutralizing the force)
3. Return (redirecting the force)

DETECT

Because pushing-hands is practiced with the arms touching, touch is the chief means of detecting an attack.

CLING

After detecting a force, one clings to it. The motto is: "Stick to the partner's limbs unless one of your own is trapped."

THE CYCLE OF PUSHING-HANDS

STEP 1: You have just completed a push. Your partner, using the force supplied by you, begins to push back.

STEP 2: Hold the force for a split second to make sure you "register" it properly and are not just responding through routine.

STEP 3: Yield and absorb your partner's push/force. Begin to smoothly borrow the force and return it.

Worshippers entering the Kamigamo Shrine in Kyoto. Kyoto is a spiritual and cultural center of great importance to the Japanese people.

If an arm is trapped, free it, and at the same time, monitor your partner's free arm with your free arm. The free hand must not be taken too far from the center, however, because your partner will begin to push there.

RETURN

Return all forces by turning at the waist, passing a force to your other hand and returning it with that hand, or soaking it up with one hand, passing it to the other hand, and returning it with that hand, or changing posture. All movements depend on touch reflexes.

TOUCH REFLEXES

Touch reflexes are immediate reflexes, and are faster than visual reflexes. (Feeling is quicker than looking.) What is interesting is that there is no thinking through or planning such a response. A visual reflex, however, has a more complex and time-consuming route to take.

Compared with other physical faculties, which can decrease by up to 90 percent as we age, touch reflexes are among the last of our faculties to do so. This, coupled with the use of techniques that operate only within the natural range of movement, means that a high standard of pushing-hands skill can be maintained into old age.

EXAMPLES OF PUSHING-HANDS PRACTICE

Face your partner with your forearms in contact at approximately the height of your solar plexus. Neither practitioner lets his or her arms collapse.

Taking care not to fully extend the arm, press smoothly forward toward your partner's chest.

Your partner detects the force and holds it momentarily before yielding to it by turning at the waist. Taking care not to fully extend the arm, he or she returns the force in a smooth, circular, flowing action. At an advanced level, it becomes possible to practice pushing-hands while blindfolded.

FREEDOM FROM FEAR

"For whatever a man thinks about continually, to that his mind becomes inclined by the force of habit, for unwholesome thoughts will grow when nursed in the heart and breed misfortune for yourself and others alike."

Harmonizing with another during pushing-hands or during aikido or tai chi practice gives perhaps the greatest insights into the true value of martial arts for the mind. Unfortunately, the true experience (being a Zen one) cannot be described in a book. Harmonizing with another during martial arts practice can only be felt. From a philosophical perspective, harmonizing with another has a greater importance than self-defense. Martial artists interested in the value of martial arts for the mind do much more than endlessly prepare for a fight they will hopefully never have.

HOW TO MEDITATE

Meditation and the theories that go with it can be difficult, to say the least, and I am aware of the difficulties a young reader may have with them. However, I think the most important thing to bear in mind is that from a practical and nonspiritual point of view, meditation facilitates

Right: Yoga is the predecessor of later Buddhist meditation techniques. Putting the body into various yoga positions is only a small part of yoga practice as a whole, and yoga practice has several categories or divisions, including chanting, meditation, and other spiritual exercises.

MEDITATION POSITIONS

SITTING IN A CHAIR: Make sure that your back is straight, relax your shoulders, and keep your head upright but in a natural position.

CROSS-LEGGED: Sit with your legs naturally crossed. Avoid hunching yourself up.

KNEELING: Sit either on the soles of your feet, or on your heels with your knees tucked underneath you.

HALF LOTUS: Place the arch of one foot on the thigh of the opposite leg, and sit with your back straight and legs crossed.

FULL LOTUS: Cross your legs and place the arches of each foot on the thigh of the opposite leg. Relax your shoulders.

concentration, and concentration, as I have said throughout this book, is vital for success in any endeavor.

The following example of meditation is basic and aimed at those with no prior knowledge of how to meditate.

Practice takes place in a quiet, solitary place and lasts for 10 minutes to an hour (or longer). Sitting either cross-legged or on a straight-backed chair and keeping the back straight, swell out the abdomen and put a little strength there, then relax. Close the mouth, and let the tongue touch the hard palate of the mouth. Leave the eyes slightly open, with the gaze cast down. Make sure that the chin is not sticking out. Relax the face and then the entire body. Continue to keep the back straight; do not sit with a rounded back. Breathe through the nose, and become still.

In this stillness, begin to "let go," first by emptying out and clearing away distractions, such as impatience, doubt, fear, even curiosity, and then by detaching from all thoughts, emotions, ideas, and beliefs, discarding all, even identity. After reaching an initial state of calm, gently focus your attention on either the feeling of the breath at the tip of the nose, or the rise and swell of the abdomen, particularly at the point 1 inch below the navel. One may also practice counting from 1 to 10, simply returning to one every time the mind wanders. It is amazing how many tricks the thinking mind will play during meditation. For instance, after having settled well, the mind will butt in on the quiet moment and congratulate you. But by succumbing to these outside thoughts, you have become a victim of classic thought-drift; you are thinking, not meditating.

If you are a beginner, you may find this tricky, as doubt and suspicion challenge your mind. And, if you are sitting cross-legged, pain (mostly in the knees) challenges even the most-determined practitioner, while your mind begins to fill with questions about just how useful it is to sit still apparently doing nothing. These and other obstacles can only be smoothed out with practice, by continuing to distance yourself from thoughts and emotions. Just watch them, and let them pass across the screen of your mind without accepting or rejecting them. As for the pain in the knees, well, it is advisable to move them, give them a rub, and then settle back down to meditation.

WHAT HAPPENS NEXT?

If you keep your concentration, your "true nature" or "true self" will appear. According to Zen philosophy, what will appear is:

"Your true face before your parents were born (meaning the real you). This true self—your natural inner intelligence—unlike mere intellectual intelligence, is the intelligence within that 'watches' and 'knows.' It appears only when your focal point of consciousness has been withdrawn from the external world of objects and becomes focused on the internal world of 'being'."

So, if you get this far, you will have entered the internal world of being (subjective realm or inside world), which is vast and continues on inside, working like a giant mirror reflecting the outside world.

The mystery and importance of the inside world is often ignored. Mistakenly considered to be a great "nothing" by those who have never traveled its broad expanses or plumbed its great depths, the world inside can profitably be compared to the relative vast space inside an atom: (nothing tangibly solid or concrete, alas for the materialists).

Within these spaces, the exciting potential of all creation exists; here we can find echoes of Taoism and parallels with the great vast "emptiness" of the Tao. In this sense, all potential exists within the individual, hampered only by ingrained habits, mind-clutter, and ill-devised belief systems.

In a simplistic sense, Zen meditation provides a means of zeroing the registers, cleaning out the "room of mind," and returning to a pure state of consciousness. Freed from objects of consciousness, we are conscious only of being conscious and are free to experience our true selves.

I hope that you have found *Martial Arts for the Mind* thought-provoking. If you have, then the book will have done its job, and I will be happy. There are so many different martial arts to choose from that this book could have been many times its size and still not have done them all justice. Besides, the real proof of any pudding is in the eating, so to truly find out about the benefits that martial arts training could have for you, I suggest you explore some clubs for yourself.

Glossary

Apathy	Lack of interest or enthusiasm
Budo	The Japanese warrior way
Chi	Vital breath or spirit
Feudal	Describes a social and political system in which peasants work for a powerful landowner in exchange for food and protection.
Form	Same as kata, except used to refer to Chinese martial arts
Holistic	A multilayered, but integrated, approach
Hsing	A diagram, pattern, or sequence of kung fu movements
Hyung	Patterned arrangement of taekwondo techniques
Ideograph	A symbol for a concept or object
Kata	Choreographed sequence of Japanese martial art movements
Meridians	Energy channels in the human body used in traditional Chinese medicine
Quan	A kung fu form in general and a fist in particular
Samurai	Elite class of Japanese warriors
Sanchin	"Three conflicts," the name of a karate kata and a kung fu form
Wu-wei	To be empty of intentions or plans
Zanzen	(Seated) meditation
Zen	Meditation and a type of Buddhism

Clothing and Equipment

CLOTHING

Gi: The gi is the most typical martial arts "uniform." Usually in white, but also available in other colors, it consists of a cotton thigh-length jacket and calf-length trousers. Gis come in three weights: light, medium, and heavy. Lightweight gis are cooler than heavyweight gis, but not as strong. The jacket is usually bound at the waist with a belt.

Belt: Belts are used in the martial arts to denote the rank and experience of the wearer. They are made from strong linen or cotton and wrap several times around the body before tying. Beginners usually wear a white belt, and the final belt is almost always black.

Hakama: A long folded skirt with five pleats at the front and one at the back. It is a traditional form of clothing in kendo, iaido, and jujutsu.

Zori: A simple pair of slip-on sandals worn in the dojo when not training to keep the floor clean.

WEAPONS

Bokken: A bokken is a long wooden sword made from Japanese oak. Bokken are roughly the same size and shape as a traditional Japanese sword (katana).

Jo: The jo is a simple wooden staff about 4–5 ft (1.3–1.6 m) long and is a traditional weapon of karate and aikido.

Kamma: Two short-handled sickles used as a fighting tool in some types of karate and jujutsu.

Tanto: A wooden knife used for training purposes.

Hojo jutsu: A long rope with a noose on one end used in jujutsu to restrain attackers.

Sai: Long, thin, and sharp spikes, held like knives and featuring wide, spiked handguards just above the handles.

Tonfa: Short poles featuring side handles, like modern-day police batons.

Katana: A traditional Japanese sword with a slightly curved blade and a single, razor-sharp cutting edge.

Butterfly knives: A pair of knives, each one with a wide blade. They are used mainly in kung fu.

Nunchaku: A flail-like weapon consisting of three short sections of staff connected by chains.

Shinai: A bamboo training sword used in the martial art of kendo.

Iaito: A stainless-steel training sword with a blunt blade used in the sword-based martial art of iaido.

TRAINING AIDS

Mook yan jong: A wooden dummy against which the martial artist practices his blocks and punches and conditions his limbs for combat.

Makiwara: A plank of wood set in the ground used for punching and kicking practice.

Focus pads: Circular pads worn on the hands by one person, while his or her partner uses the pads for training accurate punching.

PROTECTIVE EQUIPMENT

Headguard: A padded, protective helmet that protects the wearer from blows to the face and head.

Joint supports: Tight foam or bandage sleeves that go around elbow, knee, or ankle joints and protect the muscles and joints against damage during training.

Groin protector: A well-padded undergarment for men that protects the testicles and the abdomen from kicks and low punches.

Practice mitts: Lightweight boxing gloves that protect the wearer's hands from damage in sparring, and reduce the risk of cuts being inflicted on the opponent.

Chest protector: A sturdy shield worn by women over the chest to protect the breasts during sparring.

Further Reading

Chaline, Eric. *Tai Chi for Mind, Body, and Spirit.* New York; Sterling Publishing Co., 1998.

Deshimaru, Taisen and Nancy Amphoux (trans). *The Zen Way to the Martial Arts.* New York; Dutton, 1991.

Diepersloot, Jan. *Warriors of Stillness: Meditative Traditions in the Chinese Martial Arts.* Walnut Creek, CA; Center for Healing and the Arts, 1997.

Hyams, Joe. *Zen in the Martial Arts.* New York; Bantam Books, 1982.

Morgan, Forrest E. *Living the Martial Way: A Manual for the Way a Modern Warrior Should Think.* NJ; Barricade Books, 1992.

Shaw, Scott. *The Warrior is Silent: Martial Art and the Spiritual Path.* Vermont; Inner Traditions International Ltd, 1998.

Soho, Takuan and William Scott Wilson. *The Unfettered Mind: Writings of the Zen Master to the Sword Master.* Tokyo; Kodansha International, 1988.

Yang, Jwing-Ming. *Qigong for Health and Martial Arts: Exercises and Meditation.* Boston; Ymaa Publications, 1998.

Useful Web Sites

http://www.drrelax.com/judo.htm/

http://martialarts.org/

http://www.flowinghands.com/

http://www.bodymindharmony.com/

http://www.tai-chi.com/

http://www.ymaa.com/

http://www.shotokai.cl/otras_artes/introzen.html

http://www.jasukai.com/ki.htm

About the Author

Nathan Johnson holds a 6th-dan black belt in karate and a 4th-degree black sash in traditional Chinese kung fu. He has studied martial arts for 30 years and holds seminars and lectures on martial arts and related subjects throughout the world. He teaches zen shorindo karate at several leading universities in the U.K. His previous books include *Zen Shaolin Karate* and *Barefoot Zen*. He lives in Hampshire, England.

Index

References in italics refer to illustration captions